Will Rogers

The Cowboy Philosopher

In60Learning

Copyright © 2019 in60Learning

All rights reserved.

Sign up for the LearningList
to receive

eBooks and Audiobooks
FREE

at
www.in60Learning.com
Smarter in 60 minutes.

CONTENTS

1	Riches to Rags and Back Again	1
2	Taking the Bull by the Horns	5
3	The Dark Horse Hero	9
4	Common Wisdom, Uncommon Hope	14
5	More than Mere Words	18
6	The Themes of a Life	22
7	One of a Kind	25

1 RICHES TO RAGS AND BACK AGAIN

"I was born on Nov. 4, which is election day ... my birthday has made more men and sent more back to honest work than any other days in the year."

– Will Rogers

William Penn Adair Rogers – the man who became known as the "Cowboy Philosopher" – gained fame spinning his rope as he doled out homespun wisdom. Despite his carefully presented humility and relatability with the common man, Rogers was born into a wealthy and well-connected family in Oologah, Oklahoma. At the time of his birth (November 4, 1879), the city now known as Oologah was in the middle of Cherokee Indian territory, and Rogers' parents, Clement and Mary, were wealthy Cherokee ranchers. Their ranch had suffered some losses during the Civil War but had rebounded nicely and was consistently moving thousands of head of cattle to market annually.

As a successful businessman, mixed-blood Cherokee, and long-standing resident of the community, Clement Rogers was elected as a judge following the Civil War. Later, he would serve five consecutive terms in the Cherokee Senate and win a seat as a delegate to the Oklahoma Constitutional Convention. This background would teach Will Rogers both the values of hard work and public service and would set the stage for the man he would become.

An intelligent young man, Will was also highly independent. He had learned the business of being a cowboy on his parents' ranch well and balked at their efforts to educate him in schools that he felt hemmed in his freedom. He loved the cowboy life; while fully capable of bookish studies, they held none of the fascination for him that roping and riding did. Financially able to send him to the best of schools, Clement and Mary went through a series of them before Will abandoned schooling altogether. First, Will spent a short tenure at the alma mater of his father, the Cherokee National Male Seminary. From there, he attended an all-girls school at his mother's arrangement; his sister was attending and special arrangements were made with the headmaster to allow Will to enroll. This, too, was short-lived. Then followed Tallequah boarding school, Vinita boarding school, and a disastrous season at the Scarritt Collegiate Institute. His welcome at the Scarritt Institute was effectively worn out following his high-spirited prank, roping a colt on the school's tennis court. Dismayed, Clement Rogers made a final effort to instill some sense of decorum in his son, enlisting him in Kemper Military School. This ended in Will's eventual desertion from the program and running away to seek out the independent life for which he longed.

Lacking his father's wealth and backing, and having buried his mother in 1890, Will Rogers was now tasked with becoming a self-made man – and it suited him well. Since the age of 11, young Will had been entrusted with his own cattle, which he had translated into his own brand by the time he was in his mid-teens. Now freed from the structures of education, he worked as a cowboy on the Texas-Oklahoma border for a time before returning home, facing his disappointed father, and once again taking up control of his herd on the Cherokee ranch. Less than five years after his return home, however, Will Rogers found his independent streak frustrated again, as the open range which was so ingrained in him was sold off, parceled out, and fenced in. He turned southward to find an outlet for his frustration and a means of continuing his beloved open-range life.

Following promises of still-open rangeland, Will traveled to Buenos Aires, Argentina, where he attached himself to a group of gauchos who were running livestock to South Africa for use in the Boer War. This adventure did not fulfill the great promise of the advertisement, and within a scant few years, Will found himself with no remaining savings, in a country far from home, and with few prospects of recovering financially. Never one to quail at an opportunity to strike out on his own, however, Will boarded a ship bound for Johannesburg, South Africa, earning his keep as caretaker of the livestock on board. His hope was that once on the scene in South Africa, he would be able to find cowboy work there.

Meanwhile, his letters home to his sisters had become a source of entertainment for family and friends. His vivid description of the surroundings, his coworkers, and the adventures on the Argentinian range inspired the recipients to submit his letters to their local newspaper for publication. In this way, the American public was first introduced to the simple, pithy, full-of-humor tales of the Cowboy Philosopher. The thoughtful intervention of his loved ones opened a relatively consistent side income for the struggling young man. The first batch of letters was accepted, so the family began submitting batches on a regular basis and forwarding the proceeds to young Will. It was only through their support that Will was able to keep his head above water until better things came along. From half a world away, the name "Will Rogers" was beginning to be known in small, local circles, preparing the ground for his return that would come in a few short years.

Arriving in South Africa, things began to look up for Will. He quickly secured employment transporting mules. Once again, the unforeseen sent Will in an unexpected direction. While on that first transport run, before he was even able to pick up the first load of animals, Rogers' luggage and saddle – the absolute essentials for his work – were stolen. Bereft now of not only his cash but his means of employment, an advertisement for a traveling show caught his eye. *The Texas Jack Wild West Show* was touring Johannesburg and hiring for anyone who could do rope tricks. Anyone who could rope a calf on a tennis court could surely translate his skills to this job! With no background in entertainment but extensive skills in rope-work, Will Rogers auditioned, was hired immediately, and began the training for the career that would bring him back to the shores of the United States and forever ensconce him as an American icon.

Applying his work ethic and intellect during his time with Texas Jack, Will Rogers learned everything he could about the entertainment trade. Even as he had learned to closely observe each animal in his care, he watched Jack – his business acumen, his tactics to hook the audience, his flair that distracted them from seeing that his "skills" weren't quite as spectacular as he painted them, and his timing that kept the audience clamoring for more and content to pay to get it. Rogers credited that timing as Texas Jack's greatest lesson: "I used to study him by the hour and from him I learned the great secret of show business – learned when to get off. It's the fellow that knows when to quit that the audience wants more of."

Having learned how to transfer his skills from steer to stage and having saved every penny he could from the $25 per week he earned as the Cherokee Kid in Texas Jack's show, Rogers once again felt the restlessness to move on. Not content to simply go back the way he had come, Rogers gratefully accepted the well-wishes and high recommendations of Texas Jack as he headed on his way to Australia. Texas Jack's letter and high praise earned Will a role – again as the Cherokee Kid – in the *Wirth Brothers Circus*. With this company, he traveled throughout Australia and New Zealand, further refining his act and expanding his notoriety. Throughout this time, he maintained correspondence with his sisters and his father, and found his thoughts turning back to home more frequently. The restlessness was beginning to abate as he found himself free to move about while still earning a living practicing the skills that had been so well-honed from his youth. One third-class ticket later, Will Rogers landed in San Francisco and made his way home to Cherokee Indian territory.

Back home, it was as though the timing had been ordained precisely for his arrival. It was 1904, and the nationwide celebration of the Louisiana Purchase at the St. Louis World's Fair gave Will Rogers the perfect platform to showcase his Cherokee Kid character. While the 20 million visitors to the fair alone would have been a boon, Rogers' act experienced a fortuitous incident that took his act to the next, even more crowd-pleasing level: a stray dog interrupted the act and was promptly brought under control by Will Rogers' expert rope work. The audience went crazy for the vivid demonstration, and Will started shopping for a show-partner in the form of a horse. Within a year, Will Rogers and Teddy were showcasing their act in New York City.

The wealthy young man who had abandoned it all for freedom had returned home on his own terms found his unique contribution and was about to become not only the entertainment for, but also the voice of the common man.

2 TAKING THE BULL BY THE HORNS

"There are three kinds of men. The ones that learn by readin.' The few who learn by observation. The rest of them have to pee on the electric fence for themselves."

– Will Rogers

That inaugural show in New York City would catapult Will Rogers from mere entertainer to hero and iconic figure. During the course of his normal roping tricks, a huge steer broke loose from where it had been corralled and barreled into the crowd. Reflexively shifting his rope from pony to steer, Will Rogers subdued the animal and safeguarded the audience. Headlines in the *New York Herald* the following day firmly cemented Rogers in the American consciousness as the quick-thinking embodiment of the romanticized cowboy figure from the Wild West. His act gained him access into the most lucrative venue for the day's entertainers: vaudeville.

Vaudeville – the "circuit" – consisted of small theaters in most major cities (and many minor ones) across the United States. The New York City venues on Broadway were coveted gigs, but most entertainers made their bread and butter traveling to short-runs that had them performing in different cities every few days. Will Rogers was no different. In 1905, his lasso act hit the vaudeville circuit, and he rode it from East Coast to West, and back again. It would seem he had hit the big time, with his pay increasing to $140 per week, playing three shows a day between Boston and Philadelphia; a huge increase over his mere $25 per week in Texas Jack's outfit.

Back in the Texas Jack days, though, there were no agent fees, no

Teddy the pony to stable and feed. That increase didn't afford Rogers any luxuries at all. Rogers continued to hone his act, however, and gained traction on the circuit. He had learned the lessons from Texas Jack well; he observed his audience closely, noted what garnered their attention, and began working more of it into what had begun as himself, a horse, and some rope tricks. He noted that they enjoyed hearing him narrate the show; quipping when he missed a trick or explaining as he set up for a new one. This conversation somehow brought people into the show with him, erasing the line between performer and audience. The more rapport he built, the more audiences wanted.

As Will Rogers' career was taking off, so was a romance with Betty Blake, whom he had met during a visit back in his hometown of Oologah. Betty was an amateur actress in her own right, performing in local theatrical presentations. She was not, however, quite sure of the security of a life in the business and rejected Will's proposal of marriage in 1906. The two maintained a correspondence as Will's renown grew, and the two reached a compromise in 1908: Betty would marry Will, and he would leave show business after one final show to settle down back in Oklahoma.

While on their honeymoon in New York City, however, Betty saw Will's act and recognized its potential. Herself a keen observer and lover of humor, she retracted her demand that Will leave the career he had worked so long to build. In his audiences, she saw adoration, and in her husband, she saw the potential to transition from simple entertainer to respected voice. Betty fully committed herself to a partnership with her husband in both business and life, taking on the care of the home, the raising of their four children, and managing his financial affairs. Will, in turn, greatly respected her insight and implemented her recommendations for his show, the greatest of which was that he share more of his observations on life. The audience loved his vivid descriptions of his tricks and their results; how much more would they love hearing Rogers' incisive wit applied to his great knowledge of matters of the day?

Despite his disdain for formal schooling, Will Rogers was still his father's son, possessed of a quick and curious mind; true to himself, he became highly educated in an unconventional way. In his own words, his education was thus: "A breakfast without a newspaper is a horse without a saddle, you are just riding bareback. Take away my ham, take away my eggs, even my chili, but leave me my newspaper." Rogers read the daily newspaper religiously no matter how small the town he was playing, drawing morals and highlighting the absurdities in what he read. His grasp of the impact of both local and national events on the day-to-day fabric of his audience's life was immediately endearing to those who heard him. His irreverence for those touted as powerful, and his readiness to call all to account equally made him a trustworthy figure. This collaborative effort between husband and wife would be the refinement that earned Will Rogers notice as more than mere uneducated entertainer with an acumen for snaring steers.

Rogers' self-deprecating manner, awe-inspiring accuracy with a rope, and humble wisdom offered with the spice of a sideways smile earned him an offer to leave the small-potatoes venues and return to New York City, performing on Broadway in a play entitled *The Wall Street Girl*. After that show's run, he was offered roles in *Hands Up!* and Ned Wayburn's *Town Topics*. There really was no better character for Will Rogers, though, than himself, and it was his next Broadway role that would become the one for which he is most widely remembered. As vaudeville was on the decline, the *Ziegfeld Follies of 1915* opened and became Will's stage home for the next ten years. Playing his exaggerated self, Rogers became a mainstay of the *Follies*.

Rogers' persona on stage in the *Follies* resonated with audiences weary of the real-life struggles of world events. Embroiled in World War I, facing uncertainty, an economy largely altered to support war efforts, and deeply divided views on the trustworthiness of the government in their leadership through this pivotal time in history, the common man found a character with whom he could relate. Here was a man with highly honed practical skills – not a slick talker throwing around self-important ideologies, but a man with calloused hands, impressive control and mastery of his trade, and speaking complex truths in simple terms. People flocked to see Rogers twirl his rope and expose the folly of world leaders who did not understand or take responsibility for the consequences of their actions on the general population. It seemed that everyone could find something to like in Rogers' act – even those very politicians he mocked.

In 1916, among the audience members who had come to momentarily escape reality was none other than then-current President Woodrow Wilson. Learning of his prestigious patron,

Rogers began to second-guess his act for the evening; should he tone down his trademark observations out of respect, or should he boldly press forward with what his audience had paid to see? Cautiously choosing the latter option, Rogers picked apart the United States' readiness for war, inadequate training and provision of the military, and even what he saw as President Wilson's deficiencies in the realm of strategic understanding. Cringing as he awaited the notoriously humorless president's reaction, Rogers was rewarded with not only laughter from his esteemed spectator, but President Wilson went so far as to seek him out backstage during intermission and offer his congratulations on the entertainer's fine show. That enthusiastic opinion proved to be not simply the empty words of a politician. Following the encounter, President Wilson began regularly working Will Rogers quotes into his own addresses to the nation. For his part, Rogers gained a new appreciation for at least this particular politician, saying of President Wilson, "You can always tell a big man from a little one, the big ones don't get sore when you joke about them."

As Rogers' renown grew in theatrical circles and President Wilson made known his deeply practical insight tempered with wry wit, the nation's appetite and demand for his voice of reason grew. At the end of the war, in the midst of a weary, financially depleted nation, Rogers made yet another of his signature career transitions. Always putting his keen senses of observation to use and capitalizing on the resources at his disposal, he combined his sporadic experience with published writing with his common sense take on the war's end and published his first of six books: *The Cowboy Philosopher on the Peace Conference*. This single move would expand his audience, garner worldwide attention, and move him toward even greater opportunity. His voice, his wisdom, his words spoken with simplicity and authority, were an even greater draw than his mesmerizing skill with a rope; the combination, however, would turn him into a print, radio, and movie-making legend.

3 THE DARK HORSE HERO

"This country has come to feel the same when Congress is in session as when the baby gets hold of a hammer."

— *Will Rogers*

"I don't make jokes, I just watch the government and report the facts."

— *Will Rogers*

Will Rogers' print, radio, and movie careers launched almost simultaneously. The *Ziegfeld Follies* had given him the stage from which to launch a truly prolific body of work. The same year that *The Cowboy Philosopher on the Peace Conference* was released, 1918, Rogers was offered his first film role in *Laughing Bill Hyde*. Rogers was perfect for the role of the adventurer on the Alaskan frontier. Despite threats from the producer of the *Follies* that any of his actors taking other projects during the run of the show would be summarily fired, Rogers accepted the role. Will's integrity and business acumen, however, kept him on good terms with the team at the *Follies*. He did not abandon his role there but performed in both productions without sacrificing quality in either. Reminding the producer that he had never signed a contract with the *Follies*, hiring on with the show in a handshake deal, Rogers effectively slipped through a loophole in the producer's threats.

This seminal film role would lead to bigger and better roles. In 1919, the newly formed Goldwyn Studios (which would later become

Metro-Goldwyn-Mayer) offered Rogers a contract deal which he readily accepted. Moving his family and faithful pony Teddy to Hollywood, Rogers starred in 11 films for Goldwyn. Each of these silent films showcased Rogers as the slightly bumbling underdog figure, out of his league against a citified dandy of a villain. His common-sense wit and unintentional heroism would win the day, earn him the love of the girl, and would highlight his jaw-dropping, eye-deceiving prowess with a rope. This country bumpkin may not have the polish of a city businessman, the films all intimated, but that didn't mean he was unintelligent or incapable. The theme that elevated the common man and celebrated innate know-how made his films must-sees of the day.

As Goldwyn Studios faced bankruptcy in 1921, and Rogers' contract was up for renewal, he opted to strike out on his own. It was during this time that Will Rogers' best known and most enduring film was self-produced. *The Ropin' Fool*, based around the same formula so effective in his films with Goldwyn, casts Rogers as the rope-throwing, underdog hero. This film, however, is a spectacle of rope tricks and technological advancement in the industry, packing an astounding 53 rope tricks into its 20-minute run time. Touted as one of the first and finest representations of slow-motion capture, many of the tricks are performed full-speed and then replayed in slow motion. This tactic, combined with the contrast of white rope against black horse, took the nation's obsession with Roger's rope-throwing, wit-dispensing persona to new heights. Every young child cast themselves as the erstwhile hero in their own backyard sagas, roping their pet dogs while their parents chuckled and nodded agreement with the practical wisdom of the screen hero who understood their struggles.

After a season of filmmaking on his own and with producer Hal Roach, Rogers returned to *Ziegfeld*, leveraging his increased public exposure into an increased salary. No longer willing to accept a handshake deal with his employer, Rogers negotiated the highest salary granted to any *Follies* performer – doubling the famous W.C. Fields' take. In addition to the higher monetary compensation for his act, Rogers placed a high priority on the ability of his family to remain together as he traveled with the show. In concession to this, the Follies agreed to provide transportation along the circuit for Rogers' wife, three children, and his entire retinue of household pets including cats and horses. Absurd as this may sound, Rogers was true to his values; family was a priority and capitalizing on his opportunities was a trademark of how he lived his life. In return, the *Ziegfeld Follies* once again secured the services of the most popular entertainer of the decade.

Even as he built his screen presence, maintained his family, and continued to travel with the *Ziegfeld Follies*, Will Rogers advanced his print career and political involvement. It was in 1922 that he both accepted a contract with McNaught Publishing for a weekly column in their newspapers and began appearing as a radio personality in short topical shows, proffering his opinions on the day's news. Growing increasingly bold in his humorous spearing of the sitting political leadership as his audience – an economically faltering general populous – applauded his publicizing of their own sentiments, Rogers found himself heralded as the mouthpiece for the common man, and the powers-that-be were all listening.

Once again, a sitting President, Calvin Coolidge, became a personal connection for Rogers. Granted, that connection began with Rogers first delivering a scalding impersonation of Coolidge, more than implying that he was so disconnected from the plight of the common farmer and so intent on political power that he couldn't even reason in a straight line. In a weekly radio address, Rogers' Coolidge proclaimed, "Farmers, I am proud to report that the country as a whole is prosperous. I don't mean by that that the whole country is prosperous, but as a whole it is prosperous. That is, it is prosperous for a hole. A hole is not supposed to be prosperous, and you are certainly in a hole. There is not a whole lot of doubt about that." It seemed that this was a bridge too far even for his adoring audience, and Will Rogers found himself in the position of apologizing to President Coolidge.

Rogers' omnipresence on the stage, screen, radio, and print, and his common themes of political commentary, distrust of big business in a time of economic collapse, and post-war disarmament earned him increasing respect as a well-read, well-reasoned man. Political powers took note, and before long, Will Rogers found himself a friend of many of the congressmen and big businessmen that he regularly held to account. Perhaps it was his profoundly practical voice that they recognized a need for in their distanced positions. Perhaps his compassion resonated. Whatever the case, Rogers' own acumen in the realm of capitalization and utilization of resources garnered respect and placed him at the round table with leading figures of the day. His upbringing as the son of a prominent businessman and political figure in the precarious position of representing the Cherokee Nation to the United States at large gave him the finesse to navigate these new waters successfully. It can be argued that both the powerful and the downtrodden were bettered by Will Rogers' arrival in such a big way on the world stage.

Clearly understanding the value of Rogers' voice, his bosses at the *Saturday Evening Post*, where he had contributed weekly articles, sent him on assignment to Europe. He was tasked with simply being himself – writing observations on the political and cultural climate there and connecting to the people back home. In his unique style, these columns took on the format of letters to President Calvin Coolidge. Having once smoothed things over with the President, Rogers was less concerned about his reception of these "advisory" letters from a citizen. Indeed, they were so well-received that the collection was later published as a book, entitled *Letters from a Self-Made Diplomat to his President*.

With the great success of the European assignment, the *Saturday Evening Post* then sent Rogers to the Soviet Union. Continuing his signature style of critical observation, Rogers succinctly delivered his take on life in the communist country. And again, these observations and weekly columns were collected into another book, *There's Not a Bathing Suit in Russia & Other Bare Facts*.

Out of this five-month overseas tour came the quote for which Rogers is best known: "I never yet met a man that I didn't like." On its face, it is a beneficent, kind view of humanity. In its proper context, however, it becomes a classic Will Rogers biting statement about a politician of considerable power. While in Russia, Rogers had tried to secure a meeting with Leon Trotsky, the renowned Marxist. Unable to do so, Rogers penned, "I bet you if I had met him and had a chat with him, I would have found him a very interesting and human fellow, for I never yet met a man that I didn't like." His delivery implied that the man he didn't like – Trotsky – was the man he had not yet met, and once again, his sentiment was championed by his fellow American citizens.

On this wave of popularity and with the multi-faceted platforms of stage (which had now transitioned largely into public speaking engagements on various topics), radio, and print, Rogers rode home from the five-month international assignment. As he returned, he became increasingly distressed with the disconnect he perceived between the realities of life for the everyday citizen and the decisions being made by those in seats of power. The war had taken casualties both on the battlefield and off. The stock market was volatile at best and was consistently delivering losses to investors. Widespread desperation had begun to take hold. And so, the Cowboy Philosopher, truly a man of integrity, became an early celebrity seeking to use his extensive platform for the common good.

4 COMMON WISDOM AND UNCOMMON HOPE

"It's great to be great, but it's greater to be human."

— Will Rogers

"There is nothing as easy as denouncing ... It don't take much to see that something is wrong but it does take some eyesight to see what will put it right again."

— Will Rogers

    The year was 1926. The First World War had ended. Soldiers had returned home to an economy that had initially seemed burgeoning with manufacturing and exports in high demand to the diplomatic allies of the United States. The flush created by high employment percentages and ideological optimism led to the spending frenzy of the 1920s. The United States, celebrating the end of the war and eager to erase its effects on the psyche of the population, ignored warning signs of the approaching end to the high life they enjoyed.
    This was the year that Will Rogers chose to largely abandon the façade of an uneducated buffoon who accidentally stumbled into heroism. His European tour had made it more than apparent that, though he may have no institutionalized education, he was most certainly an astute observer and accurate interpreter of both the events and the influential players he scrutinized. Bringing much of that sharp discernment, Rogers embarked on what he dubbed his "Badwill Tour" of the United States. In characteristic mockery and

with pithy insight, Rogers traveled the nation presenting his political humor speech to audiences in the throes of a mid-term election season. His audiences flocked to hear him speak; tired of the goodwill tours of the politicians so disconnected from their daily lives, they reveled in hearing the candidates and the government in general derided and exposed. It is likely that Rogers' views resonated with voters and resulted in the significant loss of seats in Congress by the majority party.

From 1926 through early 1929 – following the election of Herbert Hoover to the presidency – the economy of the United States continued to expand. Having lent heavily to European nations, the United States fully expected repayment and continued loaning money to domestic businesses based on this assumption. It would prove to be an unrealistic expectation of nations that had been heavily burdened by the costs of war. As loans were defaulted on by international trade partners, demand for the products of the nation diminished. Manufacturing plants closed their doors. Businesses that had borrowed in speculation of their ability to export their product found themselves with no buyers. Everyday people cashed in war bonds, draining cash reserves. Not understanding the precarious situation, investors continued borrowing money to gain a piece of these publicly traded companies even as their real value was decreasing daily. An economic downturn had begun, and a recession was on the immediate horizon. The political leadership seemed largely unaware that their international economic policies and domestic trade regulations held a direct correlation to the increasing discomfort felt by the average citizen of the United States.

Then came the crash. The weight of outstanding loans, defaults, products with no consumers – it all became too heavy to sustain and the stock market utterly collapsed, taking with it homes that had been mortgaged, possessions that had been put up as collateral, and shutting the doors of businesses who had only operated with loaned capital that they could no longer repay. The Great Depression had hit the shores of the United States. Out went the optimism of the roaring '20s and in blew the era of vagabonds, cash in mattresses, and hopelessness. Jobs were scarce. Possessions were few. And still the government infuriated the common citizen by seemingly continuing about business as usual, offering no solutions and taking no responsibility for the role they had played in this nightmare scenario.

Midway into his term, in 1931, President Hoover – albeit slow on the uptake – began to see the need for the government to address the unemployment and poverty being fought on a nationwide scale. Compounding the economic woes caused by high speculation and the stock market crash was a drought that had almost universally destroyed crops and bankrupted farmers. While still reluctant to commit federal money to relief, Hoover did institute some small infrastructure projects to spur employment efforts. Viewing the local community as the better source for true and lasting relief of the nation's woes, Hoover established the President's Organization on Unemployment Relief, and he enlisted Will Rogers as a spokesman for the program, asking him to use his considerable popularity to encourage communities to raise monies and come together to solve the crisis as neighbors.

This invitation would lead to Will Rogers' most famous radio address, a definitive moment for the development of political platforms. Known as the "Bacon, Beans, and Limousines" address, Rogers introduced the ideas of unequal distribution of wealth and equal employment opportunity that still resonate and incite debate in political discussions today. More than introducing political ideology, however, his speech offered hope to a hurting nation. He understood their pain. He saw their situation. And he had some ideas on how to repair the damage the previous years had dealt out. He spoke to the ability of neighbors to lift one another up. He called out government officials to take responsibility and act as they were able to relieve the stressors on the constituents who had trusted them to represent their interests faithfully.

To the government officials whose negligence and slow action had contributed, Rogers said:

> Now we read in the papers every day, and they get us all excited over one or a dozen different problems that's supposed to be before this country. There's not really but one problem before the whole country at this time. It's not the balancing of Mr. Mellon's budget. That's his worry. That ain't ours. And it's not the League of Nations that we read so much about. It's not the silver question. The only problem that confronts this country today is at least 7,000,000 people are out of work. That's our only problem. There is no other one before us at all. It's to see

that every man that wants to is able to work, is allowed to find a place to go to work, and also to arrange some way of getting a more equal distribution of the wealth in country.

To the everyday American struggling, but still having a little bit extra, he encouraged:

These people that you're asked to aid, why they're not asking for charity, they are naturally asking for a job, but if you can't give 'em a job why the next best thing you can do is see that they have food and the necessities of life. You know, there's not a one of us who has anything that these people that are without it now haven't contributed to what we've got. I don't suppose there's the most unemployed or the hungriest man in America has contributed in one way to the wealth of every millionaire in America. It wasn't the working class that brought this condition on at all. It was the big boys themselves who thought that this financial drunk we were going through was going to last forever. They over—merged and over—capitalized, and over—everything else. That's the fix we're in now.

The genius and simplicity that was Will Rogers, the optimism and clear vision that were the essence of his personality, became a clarion call to the whole of America – poor and wealthy, worker and government official alike – to do what they could, not wallow in the circumstance but pull together to find a way up and out. It was an address to which his whole life had well suited him. If anyone knew first-hand about overcoming, about reaching out to others, and about creative solutions, it was Will Rogers.

5 MORE THAN MERE WORDS

"If you want to be successful, it's just this simple. Know what you are doing. Love what you are doing. And believe in what you are doing."

— *Will Rogers*

The "Bacon, Beans, and Limousines" speech opened new doors to Rogers. His unique blend of calling it like it is and yet not ending in despair, his equitable treatment of people no matter their rank or station, and his barbs delivered with a twinkle of absurdity in his eye increased demand for his hopeful voice. By 1935, his weekly newspaper column had become a daily column that was published by the *New York Times* and syndicated across the country. Called his "Daily Telegrams," Rogers' column was read faithfully by a circulation audience of 40 million subscribers. How fitting that a man whose education and wisdom came from familiarizing himself with the daily news in every small town he visited would now become part of that education for others.

In addition to his prolific written word, his spoken word was in high demand. While composing a daily news column, Rogers crafted and presented a weekly radio broadcast. Following his format perfected on the Ziegfeld circuit, he riffed on the daily news, made political observations, and related to the common person being affected by governmental decisions over which they had no control. One of the first political humorists, he regularly delivered quotable one-liners that would be repeated and popularized by his listeners, succinctly summarizing their frustrations and their hopes. His words and inflection translated into the top-rated radio show in 1935.

Rogers' speaking was not only in demand over the airwaves. He became a popular speaker at gatherings of the very types of influential personalities that he regularly derided. Bankers' conventions, political gatherings, big business conventions, and seminars held in halls of education; Rogers was a coveted presence at all of them. It seemed that Rogers' determination to treat every man, regardless of background, pedigree, education, or title as an equal not only appealed to those deemed lower class, but to the upper classes as well. His distinctive brand of honesty was refreshing to those used to the simpering agreement of those seeking to curry favor. His point of view, also, was highly valuable. To men frequently removed from their constituents or the realities outside of meeting rooms and institutions, Will Rogers was a source of connection to those they sought to either serve or control. Always willing to meet someone new, and frankly amused that such men would seek him out, Rogers accepted many of these types of invitations, gathering source material for his next scathing act along the way.

Meanwhile, Hollywood was not about to miss out on the golden goose of entertainment that was Will Rogers. Already a star in 50 silent films, Rogers was pursued for roles in the new innovation of talking pictures. Realizing the hand that he held in negotiations, and after rejecting several offers, Rogers finally signed with Fox Film Corporation in 1929 for a contracted four films. In what was an exorbitant fee for the time, Fox agreed to pay $600,000 over the course of the two years needed to produce the films. Their investment, however, would prove to be a sound one. The characteristic timing, endearing drawl, and understated delivery that made Rogers such a popular radio commentator only increased his appeal as a film actor. His first talkie, *They Had to See Paris*, became a top ten movie at the box office, and each of his films enjoyed success. By 1932, he was recognized as a top box office draw and was one of the highest grossing movie stars, second only to the beloved innocence of Shirley Temple.

Ever the humble realist, however, Will Rogers never became the over-inflated, self-important movie personality. Fame, fortune, and opportunity were all his – and all by his own adaptability and relatability – yet he refused to become anyone other than the everyman that he was. Even while hosting the 1934 Oscar Awards, he pointedly teased his colleagues, saying of their mutual industry, "It's a racket; and if it wasn't, we all wouldn't be up here in dress clothes."

Amid such an encompassing career and maintaining a healthy marriage and family life, one would imagine that Will Rogers had no outside interests. Indeed, how would he have time to entertain anything else? Yet, his love of horses, ranching, and the free outdoor lifestyle never diminished through his years of building an entertainment career. His wide fame and ability to command a high salary for engagements allowed Rogers to establish the best recreational facilities right on his own property. His home had everything he needed to maintain his skill at roping, indulge his love for ranching, and host friends for various outdoor activities. Starting with the purchase of a small ranch in Santa Monica, Rogers eventually developed a gorgeous 359-acre plot of land with a view of the Pacific Ocean. On it, he built a 31-room home, guest quarters, stables, horseback riding facilities, a roping arena, a polo field, and a golf course. In addition to all of the comforts of home, Rogers was an aeronautics enthusiast and pilot, taking to the skies with friends as frequently as he could.

On top of all of this, Will Rogers put feet to his ideologies. He truly believed what he spoke about on the radio and in the newspaper. He championed kindness, equity, generosity, opportunity, and care of his fellow-men. In the wake of a drought that swept through Arkansas and Oklahoma, he joined a Red Cross tour offering relief to those affected. He traveled to the Mississippi River valley in 1927 to lend his hands to flood relief. The beginning of 1931 found him on the ground in Nicaragua bringing comfort to earthquake victims.

During the 1932 elections, Rogers backed the Franklin D. Roosevelt ticket, campaigning and working with Roosevelt to establish the New Deal – an economic relief program closely aligned with the ideological tenets presented in his famous "Bacon, Beans, and Limousines" address. Taking a page from Rogers' handbook, the new president held his famous Fireside Chats, speaking in calm, hopeful, encouraging tones to the frightened and unemployed population facing dire circumstances. He offered practical steps forward to right the banking crisis. He outlined a plan to put Americans back to work – a key point of Rogers' speech –

benefitting the nation by not only employing the unemployed but also improving the infrastructure of the nation. It is no surprise that these two influential men were friends and allies; both relied heavily on hope and refused to crumble under challenges. Challenging circumstances only required a bit of hope, some creativity, and the coming together of the community for the common good – and a little bit of backing from the federal government wouldn't hurt, either.

The implementation of this plan would, indeed, begin to re-establish the foundation of the United States' working population and bring an end to the Great Depression. It also greatly altered the relationship of the federal government with its citizens. With the New Deal, the government made itself responsible for the welfare of the most vulnerable of its citizens. In stark contrast to Hoover before him, Roosevelt did not see it as solely the job of individual communities to pick each other up; he viewed the federal government as the overseer of a vast collection of communities, able to command and direct the resources of the whole for the common good. In this, he was in agreement with Will Rogers, and together, the two men effected change on the American landscape.

More than a character on a stage, a voice on the radio, a word on a printed page, or a larger-than-life figure on a movie screen, Will Rogers was a man who lived true to who he was and what he believed. It is this that made him so beloved.

6 THE THEMES OF A LIFE

"We are here just for a spell and then pass on. So get a few laughs and do the best you can. Live your life so that whenever you lose it, you are ahead."

– Will Rogers

On August 15, 1935, Will Rogers came to the end of his purpose-filled, deliberately-lived life. True to his loves, he and a friend – renowned pilot Wiley Post – had taken an airplane excursion to Alaska in anticipation of a Trans-Siberian flight to Moscow. Scouting routes, familiarizing themselves with terrain, and indulging in their shared love of the skies, the men were en route from Fairbanks to Barrow when fog forced a landing. On the ground, they met with local Alaskans and discovered that they only had a short distance remaining until they reached Barrow. Deciding to continue on their way, Post and Rogers lifted off from the Walakpa Bay airstrip only to have their engine falter and fail. A mere 11 miles from their destination, the pair fell from the skies, crashed into the waters of the Walakpa River where the plane inverted, and both were killed.

As word of the tragic airplane crash spread throughout the entertainment world and to the audiences who loved him, Rogers was deeply mourned. A part of the daily fabric of life to so many Americans, it was hard to imagine that such a brilliant light of hope and sincerity had been extinguished. Wiley Post, too, was the most celebrated pilot of the day, and the loss of pioneers in two fields that so fascinated the public rocked the nation. Flags were ordered to half-staff, silver screens across the country went dark in a sign of mourning, editorials were written, monuments were raised at the crash site, and in a knee-jerk reaction by studios, movie actors were forbidden to fly. Yet, amid the mourning, the hopeful words and legacy of continual adaptation to and rising above hardships continued to call Americans to follow the example left by their homespun hero.

The legacy of Will Rogers is not simply that of a gifted entertainer and humorist. The legacy of Will Rogers is that of a man who understood what is truly valuable in life and showed others what it means to live based on those values. Throughout his entire body of work, common threads run. In each of his acting roles, he was some version of his day-to-day self. It was his person that captivated a nation. The way he lived his life seemed worthy of observation and imitation. His words fired the imagination of all who heard him not because of his skilled oratory, but because by all evidence, he believed them enough to actually live by them. From his boyhood wanderings to his adventures in South America, to South Africa, and back to the United States, Will Rogers prized freedom, independence, hard work, and compassion toward others. When those values are consistently applied to life decisions, a life that draws the attention and admiration of others inevitably results.

Rogers' extensive career left behind 71 movies, 6 books, and 3,600 print articles. His radio addresses were recorded. The man himself had left the nation, but his words of wisdom remained and continued to circulate, sinking deeply into the conscience of America. He left behind a blueprint to be followed to build the kind of life that he had modeled. He would continue to spur us toward a healthy mistrust and scrutiny of our elected officials. He would also encourage us not to merely criticize, but to seek to offer solutions. He would call a nation of people who may not have access to formal education to nonetheless educate themselves by the means available to them: newspapers, radio, books, and local appearances by speakers of the day. He would, by the accounts of his example, encourage pursuit of personal joy. He would rally able-bodied citizens to do more than sympathize with those enduring hardships; to actively involve themselves in relief efforts. He would inspire hope and adaptability over despair and living as captives of our circumstances.

In keeping with the generous spirit of her husband, Betty Rogers donated their extensive estate in the Pacific Palisades to the state of

California to be enjoyed by the common citizens that her husband loved – and who so loved him. The vast resources available at the ranch include offerings of tours of the historic home, horse riding lessons, polo games, and community events. It is a fitting tribute to the man who believed that everyone who had wealth ought to share it, and that the outdoors should be fence-free and available to roam.

Today, the values that were championed by Will Rogers are as needed and sought after as they were in his time. Technological advances in the entertainment industry that treated him so well now allow us digital access to those recordings and films that he left behind. His books are still available in print, and the Library of Congress has each of his newspaper articles catalogued. His home and grounds are open for exploration and recreation. There is no excuse for those of us who have come after him to wallow in despair of the government or economics or to decry the hopelessness of our situations. With just a little bit of effort, we, too, may find the inspiration that he brought to his contemporary audience. The philosopher and philanthropist would surely be pleased with the humanitarian works that have taken his name as their own. The Will Rogers Institute has dedicated itself to serving humanity through medical research and assisting cancer patients in accessing care. The Will Rogers Motion Pictures Pioneers Foundation exists to provide financial support, medical care, and disaster relief to those in the entertainment industry affected by adverse circumstances. The timeless themes of Will Rogers' life continue today; the simplicity of the Cowboy Philosopher is applicable to humanity even a hundred years after he first took the stage on Broadway.

7 ONE OF A KIND

"Everything is changing in America. People are taking the comedians seriously and the politicians as a joke."

– Will Rogers

Will Rogers was truly an American original. Born to Native American parents on the frontiers of the Indian territory. A man of singular vision and independence who demanded to live his life his own way. A capitalist to the core, turning every opportunity to his advantage, yet full of compassion for those in less fortunate circumstances. An activist of the best kind, working to relieve human suffering wherever he found it. Influential in the halls of government, on the airwaves, in print, in film; a presence with which to contend in every possible arena of his chosen profession. He embodied the American dream and the American philosophy.

Rogers also changed the face of so many of the spheres within which he moved. He was the original news junkie, reading every newspaper he could get his hands on. In a day when the morning paper was the standard, he devoured not only that copy, but also any successive "extra editions" that released throughout the day. Convinced that the news was only fresh for six hours after it printed, he sought to bring his audiences observations on the very latest. In this respect, he could easily be regarded as one of the first proponents of our much-maligned 24-hour news cycle. One could readily imagine Will Rogers being thrilled to be a commentator or guest expert on any of our current cable news outlets, gently ribbing the absurdities of our current events.

Rogers is arguably the father of political humor as a format. The Steven Colberts, Dennis Millers, and Bill Mahers of today owe their very careers to Will Rogers' work. His pointed delivery with an edge-softening of humor to salve the wound of the offended became the calling card of the political humorist. His sense of the absurd joined with his innate kindness combined to invite those targeted to join in laughing at themselves, and maybe, just maybe, to effect some meaningful change of those laughable policies. Although the tone of current political humorists has become more argumentative and significantly more mean-spirited in some cases, this rests on the character of the humorist themselves. The integrity of Rogers' work and intent was highly effective; it invited people to the table to discuss varying points of view instead of deliberately offending and driving differing opinions farther from each other. Political humor, as imagined and practiced by Rogers, was an instrument in aid of fixing that which was wrong, not merely stating that it was wrong.

The entertainment business as a whole, in fact, was never the same after encountering the powerhouse personality of Will Rogers. The idea of cross-media employment had never been so fully displayed as in Rogers' career. In fact, many contracts specifically excluded employment in what were viewed as competitive outlets. The savvy of Will Rogers allowed him to keep all parties happy as he quietly overtook every single mode of entertainment at the time. In doing so, he demonstrated the power of an integrated voice across platforms, encouraging media companies to actually seek out multi-talented performers to capitalize on this synergy.

Rogers' example also blazed new trails for celebrity spokesmen and political commentators. Entertainers at the time were seen as simply that: distractions from reality, not people with valuable contributions into the serious issues of the day. Radio personalities were to bring dramas to life or relay news bulletins, not entertain while bringing enlightenment to a real-life concern. Yet here was Will Rogers, blurring those boundaries between serious journalism and entertainment. Instead of dry reporting, suddenly here was a voice that resonated with believability and shared the feelings of the audience while demonstrating a full understanding of the factual information. Today, it is taken for granted that entertainers of all types use their broad platforms to bring exposure to news events, causes, and injustices that they feel need attention and solution. Without Will Rogers, it is doubtful that this would have become the standard.

William Penn Adair Rogers was born into a country on the brink of volatile change. He was born into a region trying to find its role in the telling of the American story. He was born with a free and independent spirit to a father with distinctive ideas of what his life should be. From the very beginning, Rogers' life was one of adapting to change and standing in opposition to the expected and supposedly pre-ordained course of things. A trailblazer and unique mind from the very beginning, his life followed a singular and self-determined direction. Thankfully, the path he cleared has made the way easy for those ready to walk in the footsteps of such an innovative and exceptional man. In a nation that prizes personal initiative and self-direction, few offer a better pattern to follow than that of Will Rogers. He was truly one of a kind – but it wouldn't hurt to have more than a few lives lived in reflection of his.

We hope you enjoyed reading this book as much as we enjoyed creating it. If you did, the team would greatly appreciate your feedback on Amazon or your favorite forum.

Please sign up for the LearningList at in60Learning.com to receive free ebooks, audiobooks, and updates on our new releases.

Happy reading!

The in60Learning Team

Manufactured by Amazon.ca
Acheson, AB